HOW TO

PAROLE PACKAGE

Triggering Your Release From Prison!

Annala d

Editor: @Jean Mobley15

This book is dedicated to:

Women and Men who remain in captivity while those who manage the system pretend they want you to be released. This is a special dedication to my sisters at Pulaski State Prison. May you use your mind and the process in this book to free yourself.

Table of Contents

Acknowledgments ---------- vii

INTRODUCTION ---------- 1

CHAPTER ONE ---------- 3

The Parole Package Defined ---------- 3

CHAPTER TWO ---------- 7

Developing Your Fan Club List ---------- 7

CHAPTER THREE ---------- 11

Package Layout ---------- 11

CHAPTER FOUR ---------- 13

Handwritten Personal Letters from the Captive ---------- 13

CHAPTER FIVE ---------- 19

Where are you on the Parole Guidelines Grid System 19

CHAPTER SIX ---------- 23

Opening Statement ---------- 23

CHAPTER SEVEN ---------- 25

Personal History ---------- 25

CHAPTER EIGHT ---------- 27

Community Involvement ---------- 27

CHAPTER NINE ---------- 29

Social Background ---------- 29

CHAPTER TEN ---------- 31

Community and Other Resources ------------------------ 31

About the Author --- 35

Exhibit 1 – Opening Statement---------------------------- 36

Exhibit 2 – Personal History ------------------------------- 38

Exhibit 3 - Social Background---------------------------- 41

Acknowledgments

Thanks to my daughter Timmesha A. Burgess known as the "Empress" for inspiring me to develop this manual and for believing in my ability to write. You are the best!

Also, thanks to my editor Jean who is one of the best in the field of editing. You get it done!

INTRODUCTION

Congratulations to you the reader for purchasing this book. If you are reading this book, this means that you are ready to take charge of your freedom, and this book is the very tool that will assist you in accomplishing that.

"How To Prepare A Parole Package That Triggers Release From Prison," is written from experience. The author was sentenced to 50 years do 20 in a Georgia State Prison for a non-violent crime. When she realized that there were people in prison serving over ten years for lesser charges, she realized that she had to do something.

This book will chart a pathway for you to follow. It will provide examples of what to do and say. If you follow the process, you or your loved one will gain freedom. When I was captured in the prison system, I had no idea of where to start or what to even do. I invested the two (2) years of being in prison researching to determine what works and what doesn't. What I am about to share with you is not a brag, but a fact. I submitted my parole package to the parole board and was released from prison approximately 60 days later.

Like most of those incarcerated, I didn't have thousands of dollars to hire an attorney to develop the parole package for me. As you may already know, attorneys charged an average of Seven Thousand Dollars ($7,000) for developing a parole package with no guarantee that you will even be released. With this in mind, I realized that I had to learn what the parole board looked for, study their process, and what their function is. I invested every moment in doing just that.

This book will teach you the value of support documentation, and how to use social media to your advantage. You will learn how to develop exit strategy from the moment you are captured in the system.

I chose to develop this **"How to Manual"** only after I used the techniques myself and then had several others use the very same process. Everyone who has used this process has been released from prison. Follow each step and witness the results in your life. As soon as you receive the book in your hand, start the process. Don't wait another day to gain your freedom!

CHAPTER ONE

The Parole Package Defined

Did you know that most people being held in captivity could be released in less than a year if they were not waiting for the Parole Board to receive a report that indicates "Review Jane Doe?" A captured individual's record may indicate that the Parole Board will not look at them until 3-4 years out. That means nothing. These dates allow the system to lessen the work on the Parole Board as there are a limited number of Board Members who are responsible for the entire State. In this case, we are talking about Georgia, but if you are within a State that uses a Board to grant release from prison, these steps will work for you. Sending the Board a Parole Package prompts them to look at you much sooner.

Jimmy Neil Smith, Director of the International Storytelling Center said this, and I quote, "We are all storytellers. We all

live in a network of stories. There isn't a stronger connection between people than storytelling." (Source: The Story Telling Agency)

So, understand this, your Parole Package must share your story. Stop right here and imagine the Parole Board and Review Officer reading your story and being compelled to grant your release because they see you, ____________________ (insert your name). They now know you the person.

I remember asking my attorney in court, *"how will the judge and jury hear my side of truth."* You see my attorney had advised me not to take the witness stand; therefore, the judge and jury never got a chance to hear me and understand who I truly am as a person. This is what I want you to understand as you develop your parole package.

The Parole Board nor the Reviewing Officers know who you are. In the eyes of the Parole Board, you are a number surrounded with fragments of information about you the person. This information is entered into a system that allows limited details about you. It is your responsibility to tell your truth. Just as it was mine at the court; however, I allowed someone to cause me to miss that opportunity, but I took it back through the preparation of my Parole Package.

The Parole Package is your opportunity to paint a detailed picture of who you were before being captured and who you are after being captured. Now, in the eyes of the Parole Board, you must look completely different. Remember, you are painting the portrait of your life, and it must be bought in order for you to gain your freedom.

I am not suggesting that you invent a story, but rather, describe your story so that it is understood by those who will grant you freedom. I have witnessed those in captivity sending a one-page letter and never receive a response from the Parole Board. You see the Parole Board is accountable to the public. They are concerned with releasing someone who will enter society and cause harm to the public. The Parole Board must have a good feeling about approving your release, but more than that, they must feel like they know you.

It is what this book is going to teach you. How to prepare a package that allows the Parole Board and/or Reviewing Officer to be able to get to know you.

You may notice that I talk about a Reviewing Officer. You may already know that a Reviewing Officer and their team review your Parole Package before it ever gets to the Parole Board. The Reviewing Officer and their team make a recommendation to the Parole Board. If the Parole Package does not provide a complete picture of you the person, the Reviewing Officer is not going to recommend your release. And you know what they mean, just like the recommendation of the District Attorney to the court Judge to sentence you to 20 years, the recommendation will in most cases stand.

When developing your Parole Package think of writing a book about your life before and after being captured. Write the package like a story. The only exception is the personal letter that will be in your handwriting, not typewritten. This letter is the only document that will be in first person, everything else is third person. Don't worry, we will give you examples.

Let's get started!

CHAPTER TWO

Developing Your Fan Club List

If you have just entered the prison system, you are in the county jail awaiting delivery to prison or have been in prison for a while, don't skip past this process as it is vital to assist you to gain your freedom.

Contact family members, friends, and/or anyone you know that will help you. If you are in the county jail awaiting transport to prison, network with someone who would be willing to assist you in developing your fan club list. Write to organizations that assist those in prison. While most organizations do not have funds to assist you, most of them will provide a letter of support and most often have members that will do the same for your cause.

Develop a social media page and post every call for your freedom. Post videos, post information regarding mass incarceration. Right now, you are thinking, how is this going to get me released. Listen, stay with me. I never said any of this would be overnight or easy, but it will work.

Connect with that one person who will go to meetings regarding prison reform, and get photographs with those who support prison reform. Even if one is not able to take a photo with the individual, get the photo, tag the name of the event and post the information on your social media page. Visit social media sites of those who support prison reform, screenshot the information and photos and post information on your social media page. Do not forget to always post a note with the photo. Say something to draw attention to your cause. No one knows that you have never met the individuals. The key is to show others to be concerned with you or your loved one that you are imprisoned.

Have those who support you send emails to the Parole Board and to the Governor of why they believe you should be released. Post a clip from these letters to the social media site. You can choose to post the entire letter.

Post photos of the captured individual of when they were living free on the site. Choose photos that show their positive side.

Get yourself on somebody's talk show. You will be surprised at how many media outlets will give you airtime or you may consider buying some airtime. It is still cheaper to hire an attorney. If you can't do either of these, post a photo of a highly respected radio show on your site. The note attached with the photo should be a brief statement of what you would say if given an opportunity to be on the media outlet.

Start this entire process upon reading this book, and don't stop until you or your loved one walk out the prison door. There is no time for doing anything else but seeking your freedom. Every phone call must be about you working on a strategy that will free you from captivity.

Don't try and rush this process, take as much time as it takes to build up your fan club list, but get it done.

CHAPTER THREE

Package Layout

Portrait or Landscape? When developing your Parole Package, I refer to Landscape and using PowerPoint. After all, you are making a presentation of you. You can choose to use whatever method you prefer, but members of the Parole Board are professionals and will appreciate the presentation style verses having pages of material that soon seem to run together. PowerPoint allows one to offer briefs that are just enough.

Think of it as eating bite-size pieces of the best chocolate you have ever had. The pieces are so small that you don't recognize that you have eaten the full bag.

CHAPTER FOUR

Handwritten Personal Letters from the Captive

This letter is handwritten and demonstrates to the Board that you are in fact incarcerated. Remember that those held in captivity do not normally have access to computers with printers. This letter will speak directly to the Board and is not assumed to have been written by someone else. Also, this letter reminds the Board of you being a real person. The letter must state the name of the captive and their GDC number, and address, as follows:

Captive Name and GDC Number

Facility Name

City, State, and Zip of Facility

Address of Pardons and Parole for your particular state

What the package is regarding, for example:

RE: APPLICATION FOR PAROLE/CLEMENCY CONSIDERATION

You indicate parole/clemency consideration as you want to provide multiple options. If you just mention clemency, this process may take longer, or you may not qualify for it. Giving options is the way to go.

Do your homework and get to know a Senior Hearing Examiner. Even if you never get to meet them, find out what they support. You can do this by reviewing what they have done in the past, where they worked or volunteered. Send your package directly to that person as the Board is not going to see your package at the onset. When you address your package to the Board, it may sit in the Board's inbox for weeks before it is finally delivered to a Hearing Examiner. The Board is not actually coming into an office every day. The Board may meet twice per month to review and vote on recommendations submitted by the Hearing Examiners. Yes, there is more than one hearing examiner. Therefore, why not send your package directly to an examiner who is going to review it. Address your package to this person.

Dear (the name of the Examiner) (Do your research and get a name and email address) **They will give you their name and**

<u>**email, after all it's not "I Spy" nor is it confidential information.**</u>

<u>**The Core Of Your Letter to the Examiner:**</u>

Please review my Parole Package prior to submitting to the Board for consideration for release. In the event I have neglected to provide any information or details, please make me aware of this prior to submitting my package to the Board and I will provide the information immediately. I understand the parole board's decision shall be consistent with the Board's primary goal of keeping the society safe and can assure you that I am not a threat to society.

On (name the date you were sentenced), I erred in judgment and as result was charged with a felony. I am responsible for what happens to me and take full responsibility for myself. **(Don't dwell on this section, move on)** Talk about the positive aspect of you.

In this part of your personal letter say while you believe you have changed. Talk about how you have invested your time. Yes, invested and not spent. Share with how you have reflected on your past that led to your future. Talk about you and you again but try to keep the personal letter down to no more than one or two pages. One page is better.

Do not …

- Talk about why you think the system was wrong;
- Talk about your codefendant, if your codefendant is released you may say that to strengthen your case for release; and
- Try and defend yourself to the Board or retry **your case.**

Do talk about …

- How the classes you completed while being incarcerated has made you a better person;
- Where you volunteered or worked while incarcerated and how doing so has changed you, and what you learned, and finally,
- How being released will allow you to become a tax-paying citizen.

Sign your letter and date it at the end.

The forthcoming chapters will describe exactly what the hearing examiners are looking for. Hearing Examiners answer to the public regarding your release; therefore, you must give them a complete picture of who you are now. Your story must reveal this.

CHAPTER FIVE

Where are you on the Parole Guidelines Grid System

Review the Parole Decision Guidelines that govern your case. This is very important as you desire the hearing examiner to become aware of a sentence that is outside of the guidelines. We all know that most often a Judge will sentence an individual outside of the established Grid. It is the role of the Board to ensure fairness as it relates to sentencing. Know where you are, and even if the grid suggests you serve more time, remember the grid is only a guideline. It does not have to be your reality. You can always demonstrate that the public will be served best when you are released. Every captured person is a burden to the taxpayer. You must say this. You will name this section, **"My Grid Number"**

If you have never been in trouble before, say this right here. If you have, then talk about how each journey has shown you that you can and are now a better person. Speak slightly of your past that started you on the journey of crime, but then construct a case of how the system has assisted you in changing your attitude even if you are 62 or older regardless of your sentence, including if you are serving life. Use this if you are sentenced in Georgia. If you are not in Georgia, check to determine if your State has a similar constitution:

Ga.Const.art IV, 2, 2. ... The Georgia Constitution grants the Parole Board the authority to parole any person convicted of a crime who is age 62 or older. If you are 62 or older, this should be your opening statement.

Section 1 - Risk to Public Safety:

Discuss here that you are not a risk to the safety and welfare of the public. When I say discuss, get into the details, such as, "I do not pose a risk to the safety and welfare of the public as I have learned during my incarceration to work well with others." Before I invested this time in captivity, I did not understand that I am the person responsible for me. Being around others, I have learned that every person is responsible for themselves. I have learned to stay focused on what is important." Talk about how long you have served in order to learn this lesson, and what contributed to helping you learn this lesson. If you know of someone else with similar charges that have been released, use that case as an example. The examiner is responsible for making decisions that are consistent with others of a similar set of circumstances.

Section 2 - My Risk to Re-Offend Score

If your score is low, talk about this and use your low score to your advantage. If your score is high, talk about if there were a risk to re-offend score used to evaluate how corrections has rehabilitated you presently, it would show that you are no longer a risk to re-offend. Paint a story of why this is truth. Also, discuss your behavior while in Diagnostic. Note: they already have the facts, so be upfront.

This is also the section in the package where you show that the Department of Corrections has done their job in correcting or rehabilitating you. Talk about the lessons you learned in each segment of your journey that assisted in you to now walk on a rehabilitated path. Talk about the fact that you have not had any disciplinary actions against you while serving time. If you have any current disciplinary actions against you, depending on the severity of the Disciplinary Report, you may need to wait for at least six months to a year before submitting a Parole Package.

CHAPTER SIX

Opening Statement

This should be a one-page document and should be written in second or third person. It must read like a story. Use the captive's name often. What you are doing here is allowing the examiner to understand that you or your loved one is a real person and not just a number. This document may have some of the same information as your personal letter, but it reads more like a story about you. **(See "Exhibit 1" Example at the end of this manual)**

CHAPTER SEVEN

Personal History

In this section paint the picture of who you were prior to being incarcerated, talk about your family, share information regarding your knowledge, skills, and abilities. Write about your work history where you were employed. This section is a mini version of your work resume. Go back at least ten(10) years in your work history. In addition, talk about your work history within while you were incarcerated, talk about the knowledge, skills, and abilities you acquired while incarcerated. You must get the Board to see who you truly are. If you do not have a work history, then talk about being in school or use this section to discuss why you believe you traveled on this erred path, but do not dwell here. At the end of the day, you must have shown where you were, and where you are now as it relates to how you think. And, it must be a clear picture of a "better human being." This section will demonstrate to the Board that you have knowledge, skills, and abilities that can be utilized outside of the walls of the prison. This section must show that you will not become a burden to the State; otherwise, they will conclude that it would be more advantageous to keep you where you are if they believe the State will be forced to take care of you. **(See "Exhibit 2" Example at the end of this manual)**

CHAPTER EIGHT

Community Involvement

In this section, discuss any activities that involve you helping others in your community that you resided prior to being incarcerated. Talk about how the services you provided helped others. Give examples, even if you passed out bag lunches, talk about this. In other words, talk about things you have done that benefited others.

Talk about the community you served within the walls. This is not about the detail/job you performed. What else did you volunteer to do? Did you assist others with reading? Did you volunteer to anything that was not a detail? Talk about this.

CHAPTER NINE

Social Background

This section is designed to be heartfelt. This is where you really highlight your persona. Talk about your belief system and how it carved you into who you truly are. This could be one of the most important sections of the entire package. **(See "Exhibit 3" Example at the end of this manual)**

CHAPTER TEN

Community and Other Resources

Say where you plan to be employed upon your release. Say why you believed you will be hired. Talk about the position you will hold and the average income you will make. Talk about the resources you will use to locate employment. Specify a job resource site. Talk about groups that will support you, such as church groups, etc. Provide names and addresses of those who support you and provide photos if possible.

Talk about where you will live and what you will do for transportation. Provide the address, provide a photo of the residence, and a picture of the vehicle if possible.

You will prepare and include "Exhibit 4" in this package. It should consist of the following:

- Photo of the residence where you will live;
- Photo of your transportation or say you will utilize public transportation;
- Photo of the family who supports you; and
- Letters of support and/or post and emails demonstrating support for you.

Name this Exhibit 4 – Pictures, Letters of Support including Social media support.

Copy any post from your social media page that we discussed in this manual and include in this package. All letters of support must be on letterhead of the organization or company providing you their support.

Seek a letter of support from your General Counselor or from someone at the prison facility where you were held captive. If they will not give you a copy to attach to your package, ask them to write a letter of support directly into the corrections system.

Sometimes the Judge or DA will provide a letter of support, ask. It never hurts to ask for a letter of support. There are many organizations that will give you a letter of support. Write them, tell your story, and then ask.

You have read and studied these guidelines … but … would just like someone else to prepare your package for you, no worries.

Go to our website at www.dreamcatchpublishing.com and complete a "Contact Me," and someone from our office will contact you regarding preparing a professional parole package designed just for you. You may also choose to email us at dreamcatchpublishing@gmail.com.

About the Author

Annala d is a master seer and is known to be clairvoyant. She is sought after throughout the nation as she is a powerful orator and teacher. She astounds masses with her ability to communicate life challenges into a teaching moment. It was through the embracing of her journey to prison that she was able to learn the lesson on the real method of escaping any stronghold. While in prison she developed a Parole Package that caused her release from prison within 90 days.

The path through prison led her to understand here true-self and the power that is waiting to reveal itself through pure will. Annala d' does not avow her education, although she studies at Georgia State University. She is most often heard saying that living life in this earthly realm is the greatest education that one can obtain. Repeatedly, she has proven that one can escape or embrace whatever they will. It is her life's work to teach the truth to all.

Look for other releases by Annala d' - Coming Soon …

Screaming From the Inside – The Truth about Prison and how to Escape without Penalty!

Awaken On the Inside (Series)

First Class Ticket – On the Mother Ship

Exhibit 1 – Opening Statement

Request for Early Release, Clemency, or Pardon Consideration

For

[redacted]

GDC #: [redacted]

Opening Statement

In 2017 [redacted] failed to exercise due diligence in judgment, and as a result was charged with a felony. [redacted] now understands that not only should she not make decisions from instinct, but she must also include considerations of intellect and spiritual mind. At Pulaski [redacted] has completed her case plan which consisted of (1) Motivation For Change, (2) Re-Entry Skills Building, and (3) Top Step. These classes provided [redacted] the tools to assist her in better decision making, and work plans that will allow true success for herself and her future. In addition, [redacted] volunteered for details of Library Aide, Dorm Orderly, and Transportation Specialist (Transporting those in wheelchairs to various On-site locations). [redacted] five (5) year work plan and career assessment developed during the Re-Entry Skills building class allowed her to more effectively determine strengths and weaknesses. In addition, [redacted] has taken advantage of utilizing the library and the Career center at Pulaski to continue strengthening her administrative skills as well as her ability to assess various personality traits within herself; Using those resources, she was able to better determine and understand the underlying motives of others. [redacted] knowledge, skills, and experience prior to becoming incarcerated and even while being at

Pulaski has equipped her to again become a contributing tax paying citizen and no longer be a burden on the State of Georgia taxpayers who are already overtaxed because of prisons being overcrowded.

In accordance with the February 2018 Report of the Georgia Council Criminal Justice Reform, taxpayers are expending $1 billion annually for adult corrections. [redacted] has been charged with a [redacted] crime and it is believed that her release would assist to eliminate a portion of the tax burden on the citizens of the State of Georgia and help support Georgia's goals of releasing [redacted] offenders.

Your Name

GDC Number

Exhibit 2 – Personal History

[redacted] is a mother of four (4) children who are now adults, a wife to a retired 32 yr military veteran where they shared a happy union prior to this horrific experience. She is a grandmother to four grandchildren (two of which are serving in the U.S. armed forces as well). [redacted] continues to have a strong family support system. [redacted] has health insurance as well and qualifies to receive retirement benefits from the work positions in which she had vested during her work careers.

[redacted] has extensive work commencing with Metro Atlanta Skills Center where she received skills training and then began a career with [redacted] as a receptionist where she worked her way up to the position of a contract Specialist for the [redacted]. While working at [redacted] she also enrolled in the College of Business seeking a degree in Business Administration. She worked for the [redacted] for 10 years, earned her BBA, and then relocated to Miami, FL, and became employed with the [redacted] in the position of a Contract Specialist for 11 years as a Procurement Director. [redacted] attended school to obtain a Commercial Drivers' License (CDL) after which, her late husband [redacted] and she had worked for as Over-The-Road Logistics Providers for over seven years driving throughout the country before relocating back to Georgia so she could be closer to her daughter while she attended college at [redacted]. [redacted] later obtained a position with the [redacted] in Georgia as a [redacted]. She handled thousands of dollars receiving funds for the payment of [redacted], and then prepared accounts receivable reports for the budget office where she turned the cash in daily. She was given consistent bonuses because of her work effort and ethics with the [redacted]. [redacted] worked for the [redacted] for three years when she decided it was time for her to become a business owner. She conducted lots of research and decided to finally open a small business from her home in 2003 in the county of [redacted], and in the [redacted]. After being in business several years, she changed her business plan to focus attention on managing transportation companies and providing community support to youth and elderly when possible. She applied and received certifications as a [redacted], [redacted], and received her certification as a drug screening service provider.

While operating her business in the [redacted], [redacted] was very excited as a small business to do business with the [redacted]. Through her eagerness to do business with a State Agency, she failed to use good judgment in business which led to her investing time in Pulaski State Prison. After the death of her late husband, [redacted] met and married [redacted] and relocated to Alabama where she continued to operate her small business. [redacted] and [redacted] would have celebrated five (5) years of marriage when their lives would change forever. When [redacted] was imprisoned, she had 2 part-time workers, paid state and federal taxes, filed federal income taxes, and was up to date prior to being incarcerated. She also continued to hold a commercial drivers' license.

Your Name

GDC Number

Exhibit 3 - Social Background

[redacted] has worked all her life even when I was a student in college, for years as a single mother, and American citizen.

The American dream for [redacted] was to build a legacy for her children as all responsible parents hope to provide for their children in a world where our lineage was not awarded the silver spoon phenomenon. Although, raised by a single mom and 6 other siblings in the housing projects, [redacted] worked hard so that her children would not have to grow up in that lifestyle. Before spending time in Pulaski she understands her naïve nature regarding unknown sophisticated business dealings; assuming that the opportunity was a blessing rather than what appears to be a curse that has altered the direction of her life forever.

[redacted] has always had a heart for those labeled disadvantaged, and truly believed that every opportunity was established for her to help, not to be scorned for helping due to lack of knowledge (what a slap in the face some would say). In every work position [redacted] has EVER had, she earned the public's trust in which she was entrusted. She had access to hundreds of clients' financial information when she managed compliance for the transportation firms and prior throughout her career. One of the ideas [redacted] states that she now understands is,

"And once the storm is over, you won't remember how you made it through, how you managed to survive. You won't even be sure, whether the storm is really over.

But one thing is certain. When you come out of the storm, you won't be the same person who walked in. That's what this storm's all about." — Haruki Murakami **- (Note to Purchaser: Do not use this quote, find one that resonates with you, but do locate and use a quote)**

CPSIA information can be obtained
at www.ICGtesting.com
Printed in the USA
LVHW042030141019
634129LV00029B/7015/P

9 780578 583259